AMELIA AND THE SECRETS OF THE SHIMMERING HOLLOW

JOVIGA MUKUNDAN

Copyright © Joviga Mukundan
All Rights Reserved.

This book has been self-published with all reasonable efforts taken to make the material error-free by the author. No part of this book shall be used, reproduced in any manner whatsoever without written permission from the author, except in the case of brief quotations embodied in critical articles and reviews.

The Author of this book is solely responsible and liable for its content including but not limited to the views, representations, descriptions, statements, information, opinions and references ["Content"]. The Content of this book shall not constitute or be construed or deemed to reflect the opinion or expression of the Publisher or Editor. Neither the Publisher nor Editor endorse or approve the Content of this book or guarantee the reliability, accuracy or completeness of the Content published herein and do not make any representations or warranties of any kind, express or implied, including but not limited to the implied warranties of merchantability, fitness for a particular purpose. The Publisher and Editor shall not be liable whatsoever for any errors, omissions, whether such errors or omissions result from negligence, accident, or any other cause or claims for loss or damages of any kind, including without limitation, indirect or consequential loss or damage arising out of use, inability to use, or about the reliability, accuracy or sufficiency of the information contained in this book.

Made with ♥ on the Notion Press Platform
www.notionpress.com

Contents

Disclaimer

This book contains images that have been created using artificial intelligence (AI) tools. These images are generated based on algorithms and prompts, rather than traditional human artistry or photography. As such, they may not always reflect real-world accuracy, proportions, or artistic intent in the same way as manually crafted works.

While every effort has been made to ensure that the AI-generated visuals align with the themes and content of this book, they are provided for illustrative and artistic purposes only. Any resemblance to real people, places, or objects—living or deceased—is purely coincidental.

Additionally, AI-generated images may contain subtle anomalies or inconsistencies that are inherent to the technology. Readers should view these images as creative interpretations rather than precise representations of reality.

The inclusion of AI-generated artwork does not imply endorsement of any specific AI platform, and all images used in this book are in compliance with copyright and usage policies.

Thank you for your understanding and appreciation of this evolving form of digital creativity.

Author

The Call to Adventure

The village of Brindlewood lay nestled in a lush valley, surrounded by towering peaks that seemed to scrape the sky. For as long as she could remember, Amelia had dreamed of those mountains. Tales of hidden treasures, ancient ruins, and uncharted lands beyond the peaks filled her imagination. But Brindlewood was a place where dreams were brushed aside by the weight of daily life.

Amelia wasn't like the others in the village. While they tended fields and mended nets, she spent her days poring over maps and old tomes left behind by her late father, a once-famous explorer. Her favorite was a map marked with a curious "X" deep within the mountains—a place her father had called "The Shimmering Hollow."

One crisp autumn morning, Amelia was cleaning her father's study when she stumbled upon a letter hidden in the drawer of his old desk. The parchment was faded, the ink smudged, but the words were unmistakable:

"Amelia, if you're reading this, it means I didn't return. The Hollow holds secrets beyond imagination, but it is not

without danger. If you are brave enough to follow in my footsteps, take my map and find the truth. Trust your instincts, and never lose hope."

Her heart raced as she read the words. She could almost hear her father's voice, urging her onward. The map, the stories, the dreams—they weren't just fantasies. They were a calling.

That evening, as the village prepared for the harvest festival, Amelia stood on the edge of the square, clutching the map. She knew what this meant. She'd have to leave everything behind: the safety of the valley, her friends, and the life she'd always known.

Just as doubt began to creep in, her best friend, Ryan, appeared at her side. "What's that?" he asked, pointing to the map.

Amelia hesitated but handed it to him. As he studied the markings, his eyes widened. "You're really going, aren't you?"

"I have to," she replied, her voice steady. "My father believed in this, and so do I."

Ryan was silent for a moment, then grinned. "Well, you're not going alone. Someone has to make sure you don't get lost out there."

Relief and gratitude washed over her. "Thank you, Ryan."

The two stood together, staring at the mountains silhouetted against the evening sky. Tomorrow, they would leave Brindlewood behind and step into the unknown.

Amelia's adventure was about to begin.

Into the Unknown

The first light of dawn crept over the peaks as Amelia tightened the straps on her pack. Brindlewood was still asleep, its cobblestone streets silent except for the rustling of leaves in the cool breeze. Ryan yawned beside her, adjusting the sword his older brother had reluctantly lent him.

"You sure you packed everything?" Ryan asked, eyeing the stuffed bag on Amelia's shoulders.

Amelia smirked. "I'm sure. And if I forgot something, I'm sure you'll remind me a hundred times."

Ryan chuckled. "That's what I'm here for."

They left quietly, their footsteps fading into the forest trail leading to the mountains. The path was one her father had often taken on his smaller expeditions, but beyond the ridge, it was unfamiliar territory.

Hours passed as they trekked deeper into the woods. The trees grew denser, their branches forming a canopy that filtered the sunlight into thin beams. Birds flitted overhead, and the distant sound of a brook guided them forward.

By midday, they reached the edge of the forest, where the land sloped upward into the rugged foothills. Jagged rocks and narrow trails replaced the soft forest floor. Amelia pulled out the map, scanning the faded markings.

“The path splits ahead,” she said, pointing to two trails winding in opposite directions. “One leads through the Misty Gorge, and the other along the Ridge Pass. Both eventually reach the Shimmering Hollow.”

Ryan leaned over to study the map. “Mist or heights. Which do you prefer?”

Amelia hesitated. The Misty Gorge was notorious for travelers losing their way in its thick fog, but the Ridge Pass was exposed, with sheer drops on either side.

After a moment, she decided. “The Ridge Pass. It’s dangerous, but we’ll have a clearer path.”

Ryan nodded. “Let’s hope the winds stay calm.”

The climb was steeper than they expected. Loose stones shifted underfoot, and sharp gusts of wind howled around them. Below, the valley stretched endlessly, making every step near the edge feel perilous.

By late afternoon, the sky darkened with heavy clouds. A storm was coming.

“We need shelter,” Amelia said, scanning the rocky cliffs. “There!” Ryan pointed to a narrow crevice in the rock wall.

They squeezed inside just as the sky opened up, rain pouring in sheets. Thunder cracked overhead, shaking the ground.

As they caught their breath, Amelia noticed strange markings on the wall—symbols carved deep into the stone. She ran her fingers over them.

"These aren't natural," she whispered.

Ryan leaned closer. "What do they mean?"

Amelia traced a spiral symbol that seemed familiar. "I've seen this before... on the map. It's a guidepost."

Lightning flashed, illuminating a hidden path beyond the crevice. Amelia's pulse quickened. "We're on the right track."

Outside, the storm raged on, but inside, a new path had revealed itself.

The adventure had truly begun.

Allies and Enemies

The storm had passed by morning, leaving the mountains glistening under the pale sunlight. Water dripped from the jagged cliffs as Amelia and Ryan cautiously stepped out of the crevice. The carved symbols on the wall lingered in Amelia's mind. Someone—or something—had left those markings, and it wasn't just a coincidence.

The hidden path beyond the crevice was narrow and overgrown, twisting through sharp rocks and low-hanging branches. They moved slowly, wary of loose stones beneath their boots.

After an hour of careful climbing, they heard it—a rustling in the bushes ahead.

Ryan instinctively gripped the hilt of his sword. "Stay behind me."

Before Amelia could protest, a figure stumbled out of the thicket, arms raised in surrender. It was a boy, no older than them, with tangled dark hair and clothes torn from travel. His face was smudged with dirt, but his wide eyes were sharp with awareness.

"Wait! I'm not here to hurt you!" he blurted out, catching his breath. Ryan didn't lower his sword. "Who are you?"

"Eric. I was part of a merchant caravan... until bandits attacked. I've been running for days."

Amelia stepped forward cautiously. "Bandits?"

Eric nodded, eyes darting around. "They control the lower passes. They rob anyone trying to cross the mountains. I escaped, but they're still out there."

Ryan frowned, exchanging a glance with Amelia . Bandits were the last thing they needed.

“Why come this way?” Amelia asked.

Eric hesitated. “I heard rumors about a place called the Shimmering Hollow. Said to be full of treasure. I figured if I could get there before anyone else...” He trailed off, realizing how it sounded.

“You’re chasing the same legend we are,” Amelia murmured. Eric’s eyes lit up. “Wait—you’re after the Hollow too?” Ryan sighed. “Great. Another treasure hunter.”

Amelia ignored him. “If those bandits are nearby, we can’t stay out in the open. Do you know another way through the pass?”

Eric nodded eagerly. “I found an old trail, barely used. It’s hidden, but it should take us past the lower valleys without running into trouble.”

Ryan crossed his arms. “And we’re just supposed to trust you?”

Eric smirked. “You can stay here and wait for the bandits if you’d rather.”

Amelia considered their options. As much as she hated it, trusting Eric might be their best chance.

“Show us the path,” she said firmly.

They followed Eric through the tangled undergrowth, moving swiftly. The air grew colder, and the trees thinned as they climbed higher.

But they weren't alone.

From the shadows above, hidden eyes watched their every move.

A hooded figure leaned against a twisted pine, gripping a curved blade. He smirked, revealing a jagged scar across his cheek.

"They're heading for the Hollow," he muttered.

Behind him, more figures emerged—bandits, armed and ready. "Let them lead us straight to the prize."

Unaware of the danger trailing them, Amelia and her newfound allies pressed on toward the heart of the mountains.

The race for the Shimmering Hollow had begun.

The First Trial

The hidden trail twisted upward, narrowing into steep, rocky steps carved long ago. Amelia, Ryan, and Eric pressed forward, the air thinning with every step. The sky darkened as heavy clouds gathered, casting long shadows across the jagged peaks.

"We need to find shelter before it gets worse," Ryan muttered, glancing nervously at the sky.

Eric wiped sweat from his brow. "There's a cave up ahead. I saw it yesterday while scouting."

Amelia nodded. "Let's move."

Minutes later, they found the cave—a dark, gaping mouth in the mountainside. The air inside was cool and damp, carrying the faint scent of earth and stone.

But something felt... off.

Amelia paused at the entrance, studying strange markings etched into the stone. Symbols, spirals, and runes—similar to the ones they'd seen before.

"This wasn't just any shelter," she murmured. "Someone built this place with purpose."

Eric peered into the shadows. “Purpose or not, it’s dry. I’m going in.”

They carefully stepped inside, their footsteps echoing softly. Ryan lit a torch, casting flickering light across the cavern walls.

The passage led deeper into the mountain, and soon they stood before an ancient stone door, half-buried by rubble. Strange symbols circled its edges, glowing faintly in the torchlight.

Amelia leaned closer. “It’s a puzzle.”

“What kind of puzzle?” Ryan asked.

“There are four symbols here: a sun, a mountain, a river, and a serpent. They must need to be pressed in the right order.”

Eric crossed his arms. “Or the wrong order could kill us.”

Amelia took a deep breath. “My father always said the mountains were born of fire, carved by rivers, and guarded by serpents.” She traced the symbols thoughtfully.

“Fire is the sun,” she whispered, pressing the sun symbol. A soft click echoed.

“Then the mountain...” She pressed it next.

Another click.

“Rivers carved the stone.” She pressed the river symbol. Nothing.

Ryan tensed. “Uh, Amelia—”

The ground trembled.

“Amelia!”

Before she could react, the serpent symbol lit up on its own, and the stone door slowly groaned open.

Amelia exhaled. “Looks like the serpent was last.”

Eric grinned nervously. “Good guess.”

Beyond the door, a narrow bridge stretched over a vast chasm. Below, the darkness seemed endless. The bridge was old, its stone cracked and worn.

Ryan tested it with his foot. “This doesn’t look safe.”

A deep, guttural growl echoed from the shadows behind them. Eric paled. “We don’t have time to argue.”

From the tunnel, two massive shapes emerged—hulking stone beasts with glowing eyes, their bodies etched with the same ancient symbols. Guardians.

“They were waiting for us!” Ryan shouted.

Amelia sprinted forward. “RUN!”

They bolted onto the bridge, the stone guardians crashing after them. The bridge trembled under their weight, stones crumbling into the abyss.

Halfway across, the path split. One way led to a narrow, intact ledge; the other was wider but cracked and unstable.

“Which way?!” Eric yelled.

Amelia made a split-second decision. “The narrow path—trust me!”

They veered onto the thin ledge, hearts pounding. Behind them, one of the guardians leapt, landing heavily on the wider path. The cracked stone gave way beneath it, sending the creature plummeting into the dark.

The second guardian skidded to a halt, unable to follow.

Breathless, they stumbled into the safety of the far

tunnel.

Amelia leaned against the wall, catching her breath. “That... was too close.”

Ryan smirked weakly. “Remind me why I followed you again?” Eric laughed nervously. “Because you’re both crazy.”

But Amelia wasn’t laughing. She stared ahead, where the tunnel sloped downward.

“The Hollow is close. I can feel it.”

Yet deep in the shadows, something far more dangerous than stone guardians awaited.

And the true trial had only begun.

Secrets Uncovered

The tunnel walls seemed to close in as they descended, the air growing colder and heavier. Amelia held the torch high, its flickering light casting long, dancing shadows along the ancient stone. Strange symbols covered the walls—more than they had seen before.

"These markings..." Amelia whispered, running her fingers across the carvings. "They're different. Older."

Eric squinted at the symbols. "Older than what?"

"Older than the guardians, older than any map." She paused. "This wasn't just a path to the Hollow. This was a warning."

Ryan tightened his grip on his sword. "Warnings carved into stone usually mean we're heading straight into something we shouldn't."

Amelia's heart pounded. Yet every step forward felt right, as if something was guiding her.

Suddenly, the tunnel opened into a vast chamber. At its center stood a massive stone obelisk, cracked and worn by time. Around it, ancient murals told stories in faded colors—battles, rituals, and a glowing crystal embedded within a mountain.

"The Heart of the Hollow," Amelia murmured.

Ryan frowned. "What is that?"

"My father spoke of it in his notes," she explained. "A source of immense power hidden within these mountains. It's why the Hollow is so heavily guarded."

Eric moved closer to the obelisk, brushing away dust to reveal more carvings. "These symbols... they look like a seal."

Amelia's eyes narrowed. "A seal meant to lock something away, not to protect it."

A sudden rumble shook the ground. Cracks spread across the floor, and a deep growl echoed from the shadows.

Ryan raised his sword. "Please tell me that's not another stone beast." But it wasn't.

From the darkness emerged a cloaked figure, their face hidden beneath a hood. In one hand, they held a curved dagger glowing faintly with blue light.

"So... the girl finally arrives," the figure sneered.

Amelia's breath caught. "Who are you?"

The figure lowered their hood, revealing a man with cold, calculating eyes and a jagged scar across his cheek.

"My name is James. And you're standing in the way of something far greater than you understand."

Ryan stepped in front of Amelia. "What do you want?"

James smirked. "The Heart of the Hollow. And unlike your father, I won't fail to claim it."

Amelia's blood ran cold. "You knew my father?"

James's eyes darkened. "Oh, I knew him. He tried to seal away the Hollow's power forever. But now, thanks to you, the seal is weakening."

Before they could react, James slammed his dagger into the obelisk. The stone cracked, releasing a pulse of energy that shook the entire chamber.

The murals on the walls shifted, the painted figures seeming to move. From the cracks in the obelisk, a faint, eerie light began to seep out.

Amelia staggered back. “What have you done?”

James laughed. “Opened the door.”

With a deafening roar, the ground split, and monstrous shadows began to rise from the depths—creatures of stone and shadow, older and more dangerous than the guardians.

James vanished into the darkness, his laughter echoing. Amelia’s mind raced. They couldn’t fight these things. Not here. “Run!” she shouted.

They sprinted back into the tunnels, the monsters in pursuit.

But Amelia knew this wasn’t over. James was ahead of them, and whatever he had awakened was far worse than any treasure hunter or bandit.

The Hollow’s deepest secrets had been unleashed.

And time was running out.

The Darkest Hour

The tunnel twisted and turned as Amelia, Ryan, and Eric fled from the cavern, their footsteps echoing through the stone halls. Behind them, the creatures James had awakened roared and stomped, their massive forms shaking the earth with every step. Amelia's heart pounded in her chest. Every instinct told her to run faster, but she knew they couldn't escape forever.

Ryan glanced over his shoulder, eyes wide with fear. "How are we supposed to outrun them?"

Amelia shook her head. "We can't."

Ahead, the path split. One way led to a narrow tunnel that descended further into the mountain; the other opened into a wider chamber, its ceiling lost in darkness. Amelia didn't hesitate.

"This way!" she shouted, leading them down the narrower passage.

The walls seemed to close in as they moved deeper, the air thick and heavy. There was no light here—only the sounds of the creatures chasing them and the occasional scrape of rock against their boots.

"Where are we going?" Eric gasped, his voice ragged.

Amelia didn't answer immediately. She didn't know. All she knew was that they needed to find something—anything—that could stop the creatures. The Heart of the Hollow had been disturbed, and now they were all in danger.

At last, the tunnel opened into a small, damp cavern. A pool of water sat in the center, its surface still and dark, reflecting nothing.

"Amelia, what are we—" Ryan began, but Amelia had already knelt beside the pool, her fingers brushing the surface.

The water rippled, and a faint glow appeared beneath the surface. "Amelia, don't!" Ryan warned. "We don't know what that is!"

But Amelia's curiosity was too strong. She had to understand what was happening. Her father's notes, the map—everything had led to this moment.

She reached into the water, her hand closing around something smooth and cold. A crystal.

The moment she touched it, a surge of energy coursed through her, and the ground trembled beneath her feet. The creatures' roars grew louder, closer.

"Amelia, we need to go!" Ryan shouted, grabbing her arm.

But Amelia didn't move. The crystal pulsed with light, sending waves of power through the cavern.

She felt the connection—the pulse of the Hollow's heart, the source of its energy.

And then, a voice.

"You are the key."

Amelia's breath caught. The voice was soft but insistent, resonating deep within her.

The voice seemed to be coming from the crystal, from the very mountain itself.

Ryan shook her, but she couldn't move. She was frozen, her mind racing with the implications.

Suddenly, the cavern was filled with a blinding light.

The creatures stopped at the entrance, their eyes glowing with a malevolent hunger, but they couldn't cross the threshold. The crystal had created a barrier—a shield that pulsed with a strange, ancient magic.

"Amelia," Ryan whispered, his voice strained. "What's happening?"

The crystal's light intensified, and Amelia's vision blurred. In that moment, she understood. The Hollow wasn't just a place—it was a living entity, a force of nature, and she was somehow linked to it.

The voice spoke again, this time clearer, more urgent. *"You must choose."*

Amelia's heart raced. Choose?

She realized then what was at stake. The creatures, the monsters, James—everything had been set in motion because of the Hollow's power. If she let it continue, the world would be consumed. But if she used the crystal, she could stop it. She could seal the Hollow's power for good.

But at what cost?

"Amelia!" Ryan shouted again, his voice filled with panic. "We need to get out of here! NOW!"

The creatures outside were clawing at the barrier, their claws scraping against the stone.

The crystal's pulse grew frantic, as if it were waiting for her decision.

Ryan's words echoed in her ears. The Hollow was beyond dangerous. And yet, the weight of the choice threatened to crush her. If she sealed the Hollow's heart, she might never leave this place. But if she didn't, she risked the destruction of everything she knew.

Her father had believed in the Hollow's power, had wanted to protect it. But James and the creatures... they wanted to exploit it.

The time for hesitation was over.

With a final breath, Amelia made her choice.

She plunged the crystal into the water.

The world exploded.

The Shattering

The moment Amelia plunged the crystal into the water, the cavern was engulfed in blinding light. The very air seemed to crack and hum with raw power. For a brief instant, it felt as though time itself had stopped. Amelia's mind was overwhelmed, her thoughts drowning in the overwhelming surge of energy. She could hear her own heartbeat, then the distant, muffled roars of the creatures, but it all seemed so far away, as though the world had suddenly shifted.

Then, the light exploded outward, the force sending a shockwave that reverberated through the mountain. The barrier around them shattered, and the ground buckled.

"Amelia!" Ryan's voice broke through the chaos, but it was distant, like he was calling to her from the other side of a storm.

She tried to focus, to pull herself back to reality. Her body felt weightless, like she was floating in the center of a storm. A dark whirlwind of shadows and light swirled around her, and she realized—no, *felt*—the mountain itself, the Hollow, was alive.

The voice came again, louder, clearer now.

"You have chosen."

The words echoed in her mind, pulling her deeper into the vision. Amelia saw flashes of the past—ancient civilizations, long-forgotten rituals, and powerful guardians who had once protected the Hollow. She saw the rise of the monsters—creatures born of shadow and stone, meant to keep intruders at bay, but now unleashed, their hunger insatiable. And she saw James, his hands reaching greedily for the Heart, determined to bend its power to his will.

And then, she saw herself—standing at the center of it all, the key to either destruction or salvation.

The energy around her surged violently, throwing her back to the ground with a force that knocked the breath from her lungs.

Ryan and Eric rushed to her side, their faces pale with fear. "Amelia, what happened?!" Ryan cried, shaking her.

She gasped for air, her vision still blurred from the light. "It's... it's too much," she whispered, her voice weak. "The power... the Hollow... it's connected to me."

A deep rumble echoed from the cavern, the ground trembling beneath their feet. From the darkness beyond the pool, the monsters began to stir once more. Their glowing eyes flared brighter, more furious than before.

"We don't have much time," Eric said urgently, looking around. "They'll tear this place apart."

"Amelia," Ryan said, his voice hoarse with fear. "What did you do?"

The crystal had already sunk deep into the water, its light pulsing softly beneath the surface, as though it were drawing strength from the Hollow itself. But the cavern was beginning to collapse—chunks of rock were falling from the ceiling, and the ground trembled with increasing intensity.

"Amelia, we need to leave!" Ryan shouted, pulling her to her feet.

"I can't just leave!" Amelia gasped, her heart racing. "I'm the only one who can stop this!"

The voice of the Hollow surged again, louder now, and Amelia felt a strange pull inside her chest. The crystal's power was coursing through her, and she knew—if she didn't act now, everything would be lost.

"The Hollow is trying to take back control," she murmured, her voice growing steadier. "It won't stop. Not until it has consumed everything."

"Amelia, no!" Ryan shouted, gripping her arm. "We can't do this alone!"

But Amelia's gaze had already shifted toward the center of the cavern. The Heart of the Hollow—the crystal, the source of its power—was no longer just a fragment of magic. It had become something far more dangerous. The entire cavern was now a living, breathing entity, and Amelia was its heart.

Her fingers trembled as she reached for the crystal, the energy pulsing beneath her touch. She felt its hunger, its desperation to break free.

With every ounce of willpower, she began to call upon the magic that had connected her to the Hollow, pulling its power into herself.

The mountains shook as the barrier that had once held the Hollow back began to crack. The air grew dense, thick with the weight of a thousand years of lost power.

But just as she felt the power surge, something dark slithered around her—James.

"You can't control it," he snarled, appearing in the shadows, his eyes glowing with the same malevolent energy that coursed through the Hollow. "It's too powerful for you, girl. It's mine."

Amelia's eyes locked onto his, and for a moment, she

felt the weight of his words. The Hollow's power was overwhelming, far beyond anything she could have imagined. She could feel it tugging at her, threatening to consume her, to turn her into something else entirely.

But she couldn't let go. Not now.

She dug deep, channeling every ounce of strength into the crystal, into the power of the Hollow itself.

"No, James," she whispered. "It's not yours to take."

The cavern erupted in a final, deafening roar. The Hollow's power shattered the darkness, unleashing a wave of light and energy that swept through the mountain. The creatures shrieked as they were thrown back, their bodies disintegrating into dust. James's form dissolved in the light, his scream lost in the void.

For a brief moment, everything was still.

Then, the ground gave way.

A World Reborn

Amelia's world spun. The raw power of the Hollow surged through her, lighting up the entire cavern with a blinding brilliance. It was as though the very mountain was being torn apart and reborn in the same breath. Her body felt weightless, as if she were floating in the core of an ancient storm. Every muscle screamed with the strain, but still, she held on, pulling the energy into herself, keeping the Hollow's magic from consuming everything.

And then, as quickly as it began, the light began to fade. The energy ebbed, the ground stopped shaking, and the cavern fell silent.

For a long moment, Amelia didn't move. Her breath came in ragged gasps, her body aching from the force of what she had just done. She could feel the pulse of the Hollow still inside her, faint now, but alive.

Ryan's voice broke through the quiet. "Amelia? Are you okay?"

She opened her eyes to see him standing over her, his face filled with concern. Eric was beside him, equally wary but still relieved.

"I..." Amelia whispered, struggling to find her words. "I did it. The Hollow... it's sealed."

Her fingers trembled as she pulled herself to her feet. The cavern around them was still intact, though the walls were cracked and the air was thick with the lingering remnants of the Hollow's magic. The crystal, now dim and cool to the touch, lay at the bottom of the pool, its glow fading as though it had given its final burst of power.

Ryan looked at her with wide eyes. "You *did* it?"

"I think so," Amelia replied, her voice still weak. "I channeled its power, sealed the magic." She shuddered, her head spinning from the magnitude of what she had just accomplished. "But I don't know how long it will last. The Hollow is..." She paused, searching for the right words. "The Hollow is part of the world. It's not something you can just lock away forever."

"We have to get out of here," Eric urged, glancing nervously at the pool. "Before the whole mountain comes down."

Amelia nodded, her head still buzzing from the energy. She knew Eric was right. They couldn't stay here any longer.

They made their way back toward the tunnel, the sounds of collapse echoing behind them. The mountain had already begun to shift, the echoes of their escape now joined by the rumble of stone against stone. But Amelia felt something different in the air now. It wasn't the oppressive darkness they had fought through—it was lighter. Brighter. She wasn't sure if it was the energy of the Hollow fading or something else entirely, but there was a sense of peace that filled the space.

Once outside, the dawn sky greeted them with the

promise of a new day. The mountain, though scarred by their journey, now seemed less threatening, less alive with the hunger that had once consumed it. Amelia took a deep breath, inhaling the cool morning air.

“We made it,” she murmured.

But as she glanced up at the rising sun, something caught her eye—movement, far off in the distance, near the base of the mountain. It was too far to see clearly, but the figure was unmistakable.“Amelia?” Ryan asked, his voice sharp with concern.

She swallowed. “Someone’s there.”

A shadow shifted against the horizon, then disappeared behind the rocks.

"Amelia, don't go after it," Ryan warned, stepping forward. "It could be more trouble."

But Amelia stood motionless, her gaze fixed on the place where the figure had vanished. She wasn't sure who or what it was, but she felt a pull—a sense that her journey wasn't quite over.

"I have to find out," she said softly, her voice firm.

Ryan and Eric exchanged a look, then followed her. Together, they set off toward the base of the mountain, the morning sun casting long shadows behind them.

They were no longer running from something—they were running toward a new unknown, a new mystery. And as Amelia glanced back at the Hollow, she realized that whatever came next, she was ready.

Because the world had changed, and so had she.

And the adventure was far from over.

The Unseen Enemy

The figure had vanished into the landscape, blending with the rocks and the scattered trees that clung to the foothills of the mountain. Amelia's pace quickened, her curiosity piquing with every step. She could feel something in the air—an unseen presence, a quiet tension that hadn't been there before. She wasn't sure if it was the Hollow's lingering magic or something far more dangerous.

"We're wasting time," Ryan muttered behind her. "The last thing we need is more trouble. The Hollow's power is still unstable, and we need to get far away from here before anything else goes wrong."

But Amelia didn't respond. She couldn't shake the feeling that they weren't finished. Whatever the figure was, it was tied to the events that had unfolded in the Hollow.

The path down the mountain was rough, a mix of loose stones and sharp, jagged edges, but they pressed on. The sun had risen higher now, casting long, angular shadows over the land. The mountain's looming presence behind them felt less like a threat now, but the weight of its power still lingered in the air.

As they neared the base of the mountain, the land flattened out into a sparse forest. Tall, thin trees grew haphazardly, their branches twisting unnaturally as if shaped by the same force that had once guarded the Hollow.

“There,” Amelia said, her voice tight with urgency, pointing to a break in the trees where she had last seen the movement.

They made their way toward the clearing, the ground soft beneath their feet, but as they entered, Amelia froze. The figure was waiting for them.

It wasn’t a person at all.

A creature, humanoid in form, stood in the clearing, its body cloaked in tattered, shadowy robes that seemed to blend with the surrounding trees. Its face was covered, but a set of glowing red eyes peered out from the darkness of its hood, watching them.

Amelia’s heart skipped a beat. There was something *familiar* about it, something that gnawed at her memory, but she couldn’t place it.

“Who are you?” Amelia demanded, her voice steady but filled with authority.

The creature tilted its head slightly, its eyes narrowing, and then, with a voice like gravel scraping across stone, it answered.

“I am the watcher of the Hollow’s last secret,” it said, its tone soft but threatening. “And you have disrupted what was meant to remain hidden.”

Ryan stepped forward, his sword already drawn. “What are you talking about? The Hollow is sealed. We stopped the monsters.”

The creature's laugh was hollow, echoing through the trees like a whisper of wind. "Sealed?" it repeated, a mocking lilt in its voice. "You have sealed nothing. You think you've stopped what was set into motion, but you've only unlocked the door to something far worse."

Amelia's stomach churned. "What are you talking about?" she demanded again, her gaze fixed on the creature.

It stepped forward, its movement slow and deliberate. "You, girl, are a fool if you think sealing the Heart of the

Hollow was the end of your journey. The Heart was only a piece of the puzzle. The true force lies in the hidden depths, beyond the mountain, in the place you should never have touched."

Amelia's heart pounded in her chest. She felt a cold chill crawl up her spine. The creature wasn't lying—she could feel the truth of its words sinking in. She had known all along that the Hollow's power didn't just rest in the crystal, in the Heart. There was something deeper.

"The power of the Hollow," the creature continued, "it was never meant for mortal hands. It was meant to remain dormant, to never be disturbed. But now... you've unleashed it. And now, it will take what it is owed."

"Amelia, what is it talking about?" Ryan's voice was urgent, his grip on his sword tightening.

Before Amelia could answer, the ground beneath them trembled, and the creature raised its hands toward the sky.

"*It* is coming," it whispered, almost lovingly, as though it had been waiting for this moment for centuries. "The final piece, the one who controls the true power. Your journey ends here, girl."

Suddenly, the air shifted—growing colder, heavier—as if the land itself was holding its breath. The trees around them began to groan and creak, their twisted branches bending as if being pulled toward the figure.

Something was coming.

And Amelia realized, with a sickening sense of dread, that they had only scratched the surface of the Hollow's mysteries. The Heart of the Hollow, the creatures, the crystal—it had all been a distraction. There was something much worse buried in the depths, something far more dangerous.

“Run!” she screamed.

But it was already too late.

The Reckoning

The ground trembled again, more violently this time, and the creature's glowing eyes gleamed with twisted satisfaction. The trees around them seemed to bend toward the figure, their branches twisting unnaturally, as though drawn by an unseen force. The wind howled, and a sudden, oppressive silence followed, broken only by the creature's low, mocking laughter.

Amelia's pulse quickened. Whatever was coming, it was beyond anything they had faced so far. The Hollow's power was awakening once again, but not in the way they had imagined. They had disturbed something ancient—something that was never meant to be released.

"Amelia, we have to move!" Ryan shouted, his voice urgent, as he grabbed her arm.

But Amelia couldn't tear her gaze from the creature. There was something about it, something that unsettled her to the core. It wasn't just a guardian of the Hollow—it *was* the Hollow, or at least a part of it, bound to protect the secrets hidden deep within the land.

"I've been waiting for this moment for so long," the creature whispered, its voice dripping with malice. "You think you've sealed the Heart of the Hollow, but the real power was never in the Heart. It was in me."

Amelia's blood ran cold as the creature raised its hands to the sky, its voice rising with unnatural power. "The True Hollow," it murmured, and the world seemed to hold its breath. "It is time to awaken."

Suddenly, the earth split open. A deep, guttural roar echoed from the very depths of the mountain, as though the land itself were being torn apart. The ground cracked and split, sending waves of dust and debris shooting into the air. Amelia stumbled back, her heart racing as she realized the true scale of what they had unleashed.

The Hollow wasn't just a place or a force—it was an entity, a living thing, older than any civilization, and it had been sleeping for centuries, waiting for the moment to rise again.

Amelia's eyes widened as the ground before them cracked open, revealing a massive chasm. From within the darkness, a shadowy figure began to emerge—a creature of immense size, its body composed of swirling darkness and jagged rock. Its eyes glowed with the same malevolent energy as the creature that stood before them.

"That..." Amelia gasped. "That's the *true* heart of the Hollow."

The creature that had been watching them grinned, its eyes flashing. "Indeed," it said. "And now, it will claim its rightful place in the world. All that you've done—your journey, your victories—they were nothing more than a prelude to this. A sacrifice to awaken the True Hollow."

The shadowy figure rose higher, its form shifting and warping, as though it were made of pure darkness. Its massive claws scraped against the stone, sending tremors through the earth.

"Amelia, we need to stop it!" Ryan cried.

But Amelia felt a strange pull, a connection to the creature. She realized, with a sickening clarity, that it wasn't just a monster. It was a reflection of the Hollow's power—a reflection of her own choices. The true heart of the Hollow had been waiting for someone to awaken it, someone to guide it back into the world. And now, that someone was her.

She took a step forward, her heart pounding. "I—I don't know if I can stop it."

"We have to try," Ryan said, his voice resolute.

Amelia glanced back at the creature that had been watching them, the one who had set everything into motion. "You knew this would happen, didn't you?" she said, her voice trembling with fury.

The creature's grin widened. "Of course. I have been bound to the Hollow for ages. I have watched it grow, fester, and wait for the one who would unlock its power. And now, you've done just that."

Amelia closed her eyes, her mind racing. The creature, the Hollow, the monsters—it was all connected. But how? How could she stop it?

She reached for the crystal, the only piece of the Hollow's power that still remained. It was still in her possession, still pulsing with the magic she had drawn from the Heart. She had thought it was over, but now she knew—this was only the beginning.

"Amelia, what are you doing?" Ryan shouted as she raised the crystal high, her fingers glowing with the magic that had once sealed the Hollow.

"I don't know if it will work," she said, her voice uncertain. "But I have to try."

The crystal pulsed with light, its energy thrumming through her body, connecting her once more to the Hollow. She could feel the mountain, feel the power within it, surging toward her. The earth groaned, and the shadows around them seemed to move with purpose.

"Amelia!" Ryan shouted again, his voice strained with panic.

But Amelia focused. She had to, or everything would be lost. She had awakened the Hollow once—now she would have to control it.

The ground cracked open wider as the massive creature, the heart of the Hollow, moved toward them. But Amelia wasn't afraid. Not anymore.

She extended her hand, feeling the energy coursing through her, and spoke one word.

"*Enough.*"

The earth rumbled, and the shadowy creature stopped. The air seemed to freeze as Amelia's power surged through the mountain, binding the Hollow's heart to her will. She could feel its struggle, its hunger—but she held firm.

"*I am the Hollow now,*" Amelia whispered, her voice steady and strong. "*And you will not destroy the world again.*"

The creature's glowing eyes flickered, its massive body trembling as though trying to resist. But it was no use. The power of the Hollow had chosen her. And with that final push, Amelia sealed the creature away once more, locking it deep within the earth.

The ground fell silent. The shadows faded. And for the first time in what felt like forever, Amelia breathed freely.

Ryan and Eric rushed to her side, their faces filled with disbelief and relief.

"It's over," Ryan said, his voice quiet, as though he

couldn't quite believe it.

Amelia nodded, her body drained from the effort. The mountain around them seemed still—peaceful, even. She had done it. She had saved them all. But at what cost? The Hollow had nearly consumed her, and in a way, she had become part of it. The world had changed, but she wasn't sure if she had changed with it.

"Is it truly over?" Eric asked, his voice uncertain.

Amelia didn't answer immediately. She knew the answer. The Hollow's power would always linger, always be a part of her. But for now, the world was safe. For now, the adventure was over.

Or so she thought.

www.ingramcontent.com/pod-product-compliance
Lightning Source LLC
LaVergne TN
LVHW021306160826
845679LV00001B/236